ISBN 978-1-333-96726-0
PIBN 10684903

1 MONTH OF
FREE
READING

at

www.ForgottenBooks.com

By purchasing this book you are eligible for one month membership to ForgottenBooks.com, giving you unlimited access to our entire collection of over 700,000 titles via our web site and mobile apps.

To claim your free month visit:

www.forgottenbooks.com/free684903

English
Français
Deutsche
Italiano
Español
Português

www.forgottenbooks.com

Mythology Photography **Fiction**
Fishing Christianity **Art** Cooking
Essays Buddhism Freemasonry
Medicine **Biology** Music **Ancient
Egypt** Evolution Carpentry Physics
Dance Geology **Mathematics** Fitness
Shakespeare **Folklore** Yoga Marketing
Confidence Immortality Biographies
Poetry **Psychology** Witchcraft
Electronics Chemistry History **Law**
Accounting **Philosophy** Anthropology
Alchemy Drama Quantum Mechanics
Atheism Sexual Health **Ancient History**
Entrepreneurship Languages Sport
Paleontology Needlework Islam
Metaphysics Investment Archaeology
Parenting Statistics Criminology
Motivational

EDITORIAL—

"GLORY TO GOD."

By PRESIDENT RICHARD E. FOLLAND

"GLORY to God in the highest, and on earth peace, good will toward men," was the message of the angel host at the time of the birth of Christ. In spite of our troublous times this message still holds good. Jesus Christ did teach the Gospe of Peace. Few there were who actual practised His teachings.

"Mormons" or members of the Churc of Jesus Christ of Latter-day Saints clair

Josephine H.. Bonnie, President, Jo Ann and E eanor Folland.

to be teaching the fulness of the Gospel of Jesus Christ. This is no idle claim, but, "by their fruits ye shall know them." We cannot teach the Gospel by talk alone— "Faith without works is dead, being alone." We cannot have "Peace on Earth without "good will toward men"—an good will toward men begins right in ou own homes, our own neighbourhood, ou own church.

(Continued on page 192.)

Cumorah's Southern Messenger

Published Monthly by the Church of Jesus Christ of Latter-Day Saints, Main and Grove Roads, Mowbray, C.P., South Africa. Registered at G.P.O. as a Newspaper. Subscription 3/- per year.

Volume 16	DECEMBER, 1942	Number 12

Editor: RICHARD E. FOLLAND.

CONTENTS

COVER

" They Presented Unto Him Gifts—" is the title of the beautiful and expressive plaque, which adorns the rear wall of the Mowbray Chapel. The Christ child is the most priceless treasure we have ever been given. At Christmas time, especially, our thoughts revert to the birth of Christ and to His teachings.

THE MESSAGE UNHEEDED

WHAT PRICE MUST MEN PAY FOR WORLD PEACE?

By PRES. DAVID O. McKAY

" And the angel said unto them, Fear not: for, behold, I bring you good tidings of great joy, which shall be to all people.

For unto you is born this day in the city of David a Saviour, which is Christ the Lord.

And suddenly there was with the angel a multitude of the heavenly host praising God, and saying,   ,

Glory to God in the highest, and on earth peace, good will toward men."

SUCH is the simple account of the greatest event in all history, save one, the resurrection of our Lord and Saviour Jesus Christ.

This is an unusual Christmastide. True, as heretofore, we send our gifts and hearty good wishes; bedeck Christmas trees with brilliant lights and sparkling ornaments; we ring the bells, and sing sweet carols and hymns of praise—but underneath it all there is a heaviness in our hearts not hitherto experienced, for soldiers ruthlessly slain by treacherous foes. As never before in our lifetime, we sense a nearness of submarines and death-dealing bombs. Devilry is rampant throughout the nations, and hate, avarice, ambition, perfidy and pride like a fearful flood of destruction threaten to inundate the world. Leaders of some nations have not only rejected, but have denounced the Prince of Peace, and are worshipping the god of war.

Yes, this is an unusual Christmastide, and our celebration is not without alloy. But as gold seven times tried is freed from dross, so may we in the furnace of trial and tribulation have our minds so purified that we may discern more clearly between the destructive forces of Evil, and the peace-producing principles of the Glad Tidings heralded at the birth of the Babe of Bethlehem.

May our eyes be thus opened and our hearts properly attuned in our worship this day.

For nineteen hundred years, the birth of the Saviour of the world has been celebrated by millions, but the acceptance of the principles of the glad tidings heralded by the heavenly host has been more of a pretence than a reality. The message of the Gospel —glad tidings of great joy which is unto all peoples—has gone unheeded! For many years, thinking men have deplored this digression from and lack of interest in religion and the Gospel of Christ, and have warned the world of its dire consequences.

Here is one writer who said, in about 1910, " Our civilization is imperiled to-day simply because it is ill-balanced. Our spiritual culture lags so far behind our material culture in its development that we have no adequate control over the latter. Our science, our education, and our government can do much to help correct this lag in our spiritual development. But in the main this must be done, if done at all, by religion and by the Church. For religion is the creator and the conservator of our social ideals; and the Church is their chief propagator."

In this same strain, Dr. Charles A. Ellwood, Ph.D., Professor of Sociology, University of Missouri, declares :—

" Europe, at least, has cause to be alarmed over its spiritual condition, but it seems at a loss to find a remedy. Meanwhile Italy has abolished all freedom of thought within its borders, while Russia officially sanctions irreligion and approves a system of sex relations lower than any sanctioned by the lowest African tribe. The paleolithic savages, so far as we know, had no such practices. Yet Europe remains unwilling to examine its ideals in the light of social facts; and to confirm N. Benda's charge, that it has been betrayed by intellectual classes, one has only to note how a plenty of intellectuals can be found to affirm that Italy is all right, or that Russia is all right, or that Germany is all right; just as we have in this country those who affirm that the United States is all right. It seems impossible at the present moment for the thinkers of the world to divorce themselves from partisanship."

Along that line a Professor Whitehead says : " On the whole, during many generations there has been a gradual decay of religious influence in European civilization. Each revival touches a lower peak than its predecessor, and each period of slackness a lower depth. The average curve marks a steady fall in religious tone. Religion is tending to degenerate into a decent formula wherewith to embellish a comfortable life."

The Gospel of Jesus Christ looks to the establishment of the Kingdom of God which shall make of humanity one large family of genuine love and good will among all its members. Such a kingdom cannot be established by force or authority, but a new life within the individual soul.

In the story of the birth of Jesus we are told that there were with the angels a multitude of the heavenly host, praising God and saying : " Glory to God in the highest, and on earth, peace, good will toward men." In that announcement are implied—I say implied, almost definitely stated—three guiding principles to the realization of the establishing of the Kingdom of God.

FIRST, is an acknowledgment of the existence of Deity to whom we shall give glory and honour.

SECOND, is the establishment of peace through individual righteousness (I cannot think of peace coming in any other way, can you?). Such a peace will result in the THIRD principle, the brotherhood of man.

Will you join with me as we consider these fundamentals :

Our faith in God springs from the heart; it is yours, it is mine. It cannot be other than personal. Jesus said the poor in spirit should possess the Kingdom of God. Who are the poor in spirit? Those who, in deepest consciousness, realize their need of spiritual possessions, not earthly possessions; those who yearn to be in harmony with God and His teachings. Again he said that it is the pure in heart who shall see God. It is the peace-makers who shall be called the children of God. " He that cometh to God must believe that He is and that He is a rewarder of them that diligently

seek Him."

What does such a faith as that mean?— the Lord becomes the centre of our being, the guide to our thoughts and acts. Men must feel that around and over all there is our Father, " Lord of Heaven and earth." They must have a faith that this universe is not left to the guidance of an irrational and random chance, but on the contrary, is ordered and controlled by a divine intelligence and wisdom.

In support of this first fundamental truth heralded as Glad Tidings at the birth of Jesus, we hear these unwavering testimonies—this from one outside: " God and the unseen world are not merely objects of surmise. We know them in experience . . . It is the eye of faith that sees the broad horizons, the colour and the gleam. Religion standing on the known experience of the race makes this one bold and glorious affirmation. She asserts that this **Power** that makes for truth, for beauty, for goodness **is not less personal than we.** This leap of faith is justified, because God cannot be less than the greatest of His works; the Cause must be adequate to the effect. When therefore we call God personal, we have interpreted Him by the loftiest symbol we have. He may be infinitely more, He cannot be less. When we call God a spirit, we use the clearest lens we have to look at the Everlasting. As Herbert Spencer has so well said: " The choice is not between a personal God and something lower, but between a personal God and something higher."

But hear the direct testimony of Joseph Smith about the reality of God as a personal being :

" When the light rested upon me I saw two Personages whose brightness and glory defy all description, standing above me in the air. One of them spake unto me, calling me by name, and said, pointing to the other—' This is my Beloved Son. Hear Him '."

Young man, " if science says to you that it has not found a divine personal being, nor the soul of man, you are not justified in concluding that these realities do not exist. There is not a single scientific specialist of repute," says Dr. Hudson, " what has at-

(Continued on page 190.)

HOW THE PIONEERS CELEBRATED CHRISTMAS

By E. CECIL McGAVIN

CHRISTMAS always had a strong appeal to the Pioneers and was observed by them no matter what their conditions were. During the autumn of 1847, the harvest was so meagre in Salt Lake Valley that no special Thanksgiving service was held, yet the Pioneers did not fail to remember Christmas. Though food supplies were scarce, and their reasons for merriment were limited, yet Lorenzo D. Young wrote of that first Christmas the Pioneers spent in the Salt Lake Valley:

I gave a Christmas dinner . . . The occasion was a most pleasant one and the day was spent in social chat, singing, etc. A prayer was offered by Brother Grant. Brother Brigham and his quorum were remembered in particular. My house was dedicated to the Lord.

During the Christmastide in 1847, it was written in the *Journal History* concerning the Church members in Iowa:

Friday, December 24. President Young and party proceeded to Miller's Hollow (now Council Bluffs, Iowa) where the brethren had built a log house, forty by sixty feet, capable of seating about one thousand persons. The house was dedicated by Elder Orson Pratt as a house of prayer and thanksgiving. The congregation was addressed by Elders Wilford Woodruff and Orson Pratt, and in the afternoon by Elders Amasa M. Lyman, Geo. A. Smith, and President Young. Elder Wm. I. Appleby preached during the evening service.

Saturday, December 25. The Council went to the Log Tabernacle in Miller's Hollow, Iowa, and attended conference meeting. . . .

December 26. Elder Orson Pratt met with the saints in St. Louis, Mo., when they donated $705.84 to assist the Presideney of the Church to remove to Great Salt Lake Valley.

On Christmas day, 1849, a gay party was held in President Brigham Young's home. One hundred and fifty persons had been invited for the occasion. " The tables were twice filled by the company " we read, " and all were feasted with the good things of the valley. When the tables were removed, dancing commenced, which was continued with energy and without interruption, except for supper, till a late hour."

At the same time in Kanesville, Iowa, a similar social was held. " In the evening we had a little sociable dance," we read, " the party being composed mostly of Philadelphians."

On December 25, 1851, Captain Pitt's band, consisting of twenty-six members, promenaded the streets of Salt Lake City " and played before the houses of the First Presidency, the Twelve Apostles and others, while riding on horseback.

The *Journal History* contains a complete and interesting account of the celebration at Christmas time in 1851, from whom we quote:

Christmas Day. Fine weather prevailed in Great Salt Lake City. All the hands engaged on the public works attended a picnic party in the Carpenter's Shop on the Temple Block which was cleared and decorated for the occasion. Several hundred persons attended and enjoyed themselves in both dance and song. President Brigham Young was also present. The enjoyments were varied with songs and addresses. The brethren of the band serenaded the inhabitants of the City from midnight till daylight which was quite a treat.

Elder George D. Watt gives the following account of these Christmas festivities:

Early on Christmas morning, Thursday,

December 25, several companies of serenaders, with brass instruments made the sleeping mountains echo with the sound of rejoicing . Our attention was drawn more particularly to the Governor's mansion, in the front of which was drawn up in military order a troop of horsemen. This was the brass band, giving His Excellency a good wish in sweet strains.

At ten o'clock a.m., the committee of management was in respectful waiting to receive those who were invited to the party. The carpenter's hall, one hundred feet long and thirty-two feet wide, is admirably adapted for a mammoth party, which was comfortable, and suitably decorated for the occasion. Now the merry workmen, with their happy wives, and smiling daughters, clad in genteel apparel, some pouring in from every quarter, loaded with an abundance of luxuries of every description which were deposited in an adjoining hall, called the machine room, which is forty feet square, in which also was situated the ladies' dressing room.

At 11 o'clock the house was called to order, and a suitable prayer and thanksgiving was offered up to the Donor of all good by Bishop N. H. Felt. The band then struck up a merry tune, and His Excellency, Governor Young, and Hon. H. C. Kimball, and other distinguished personages led off the first dance.

The excellent order, the quick succession of dances do great honour to the managers. We counted from ninety-six persons to one hundred forty-four persons upon the floor at once. These were set in order in the same time that we have seen four cotillions in other parties. There was no confusion, no dissatisfied looks, no complaining, but the day passed in peace and happy merriment, with thanksgiving to the Father of all our mercies. . . .

The atmosphere of our hall was not polluted with tobacco fumes, or the stench of the drunkard's breath. No! We breathed the pure mountain air, drank of the mountain stream, and ate of the produce of the mountains' valleys, we thought on the gloomy past, and the glorious present, and perspective future, every heart beat high with gratitude and gladness,

and every countenance was lit up with the bright fire of enduring friendship.

About seven p.m. a few songs were sung by sundry individuals, one in particular called up feelings not strange to us was sung by Phinehas H. Young, entitled " Farewell to Nauvoo." This song gave the company an ample opportunity of comparing the present with the past.

Governor Young arose to address the meeting, and congratulated the assembly on their present situation and blessings as a people.

On Friday evening, December 26, the " public hands " again met in the Carpenters' Shop where " dancing was kept up with great spirit until midnight when all separated highly delighted with their Christmas festivities. In the course of the evening Willard Richards spoke of the difference between this evening and the 27th of June, 1844, when the tragedy at Carthage, Illinois, took place."

Elder George D. Watt gives the following account of this festival :

The seats in the Carpenters' Hall were filled by the not to be surpassed fair daughters of Zion, and the brave hearted sons of God.

The company was called to order, and prayer was offered up by A. H. Raleigh. The dancing was conducted as on the previous day, and the same good order, joy, and hilarity was manifested.

After the hall was illuminated, the company was treated to a feast in the shape of vocal and instrumental music by Mr. John Kay, his lady and two daughters, the one performed well on the Guitar, and the other on the Tambourine, at the same time accompanying their instruments with their voices, this with the sweet voice of Mrs. Kay, and the deep bass of Mr. Kay produced a species of harmony highly delightful to the ear. The performance was much applauded. Brother Kay sang the Seer, in his usual pathos and sweetness, which drew from President Richards a few touching remarks. Elder George A. Smith also addressed the meeting for a short time, after which the dance was resumed, and continued until 10 o'clock p.m. A vote of thanks was moved for

(Continued on page 192.)

SUNDAY SCHOOL SACRAMENT GEM AND CONCERT RECITATIONS FOR DEC., 1942

SACRAMENT GEM.

'Twas Jesus died on Calvary,
   That all thro' Him might ransomed be;
Then sing hosannas to His name:
   Let heav'n and earth His love proclaim.

GOSPEL DOCTRINE.

For behold, this is my work and my glory—to bring to pass the immortality and eternal life of man.—Moses, Chapter 1, verse 39.

GOSPEL MESSAGE.

For the power is in them wherein they are agents unto themselves, and inasmuch as men do good they shall in no wise lose their reward.

Doctrine and Covenants, Section 58, verses 27 and 28.

SENIORS.

" Still, as of old,
Man by himself is priced.
For thirty pieces Judas sold
Himself, not Christ."

JUNIORS.

If any of you lack wisdom let him ask of God that giveth to all men liberally, and upbraideth not; and it shall be given him.—James, Chapter 1, verse 5.

INTERMEDIATE CLASSES.

Every man receiveth wages of him whom he listeth to obey.—Alma, Chapter 3, verse 27.

PRIMARY.

" Teach me, dear Father, to freely forgive
All who may seem unkind to me."

KINDERGARTEN.

When little baby Jesus,
Came on the earth to dwell,
A lovely star up in the sky
The happy news did tell.

BRANCH TEACHERS' MESSAGE FOR DECEMBER, 1942

THE STRANGER WITHIN OUR GATES

TROOPS and civilians are pouring into our various communities or nearby metropolitan centres by the thousands. With them they may be expected to bring their own ideas of community, social, and religious life. Their habits, customs, likes, and dislikes will now become an integral part of their new surroundings and associations.

It is well to recognize, however, that while they are bringing their influence to bear upon us, we, likewise, are making impressions upon them. In this duel of influences, which will be the victor? Shall we be persuaded to their ideas or will they learn to appreciate our way of life?

When this great struggle is over and we again adjust ourselves to normal life will those who have had the contact with members of the Church be missionaries in defence of our ideals or parade before the world our personal indifference and disobedience to the gospel standards? Will even one among them falter in his search for truth because of our actions?

Thousands of persons who have never experienced this contact before, will now be exposed to the Church, through its membership. What will they think or say of the Church because of their experiences with us?

Membership in the Church imposes a tremendous responsibility. We have covenanted with God that we will live by His word. What the stranger sees us do will live longer in his memory than that which he hears us say. Actions speak louder than words.

If Latter-day Saints will but live close to God, teaching the gospel through their righteous lives, it is safe to assume that the stranger within our gates will at least appreciate our associations and admire the standards and ideals of the Church. To so live is our bounden duty.

The spirit of the gospel suggests that all be made welcome. Loyalty demands that "your light so shine before men, that they may see your good works, and glorify your Father which is in heaven." (Matthew 5 :16.)

FORGIVENESS

By ELDER BRYANT S. HINCKLEY

THE greatness of the Master's character is impressively revealed in His forgiveness of His enemies. Forgiveness is always a sign of moral grandeur. It is an expression of nobility. Resentment, revenge and retaliation are natural and easily cultivated and the provocation for their cultivation often occurs but the world recognizes that there is something superior in the character that refuses to cherish them.

Paul said, " If thine enemy hunger, feed him; if he thirst, give him drink, for in so doing thou shalt heap coals of fire upon his head." (Romans 12 :20.)

So has President Heber J. Grant.

Lincoln had this noble quality in a marked degree. Lincoln said, " You have more of the feeling of personal resentment than I have. Perhaps I have too little of it, but I never thought it paid."

Divine forgiveness and a human willingness to forgive others are joined together. Mercy received ought to manifest itself in mercy shown. " If ye forgive men their trespasses your Heavenly Father will also forgive you."

An exquisitely touching example of forgiveness is dramatically told in Genesis 50 :15-20:

" And when Joseph's brethren saw that their father was dead, they said, Joseph will peradventure hate us, and will certainly requite us all the evil which we did unto him.

" And they sent a messenger unto Joseph saying, Thy father did command before he died, saying,

" So shall ye say unto Joseph, Forgive, I pray thee now, the trespass of thy

(Continued on page 196.)

The Message Unheeded.—From page 185.

tempted to prove by scientific method that what science cannot demonstrate is thereby disproved."

I know, as a very forceful English writer has said: " There are tens of thousands of bright and agreeable young people in every Christian country who do not even try to believe in Christ, and would regard it as positively eccentric to do so. They would as soon believe in Father Christmas. They have no particular foundation for their skepticism. They certainly haven't made a careful study of the documents, and most of them would be completely floored if you asked them to name a single passage in the Gospels which can legitimtely be regarded as fake. All they can say is, vaguely, that obviously the whole thing is impossible and they leave it at that." But the fact remains that " the man who has even for one second believed in Christ, will never be quite the same again. Of course, you cannot prove the power of faith any more than you can prove the beauty of the sunset. Before you can even attempt to discuss faith, you must lead your reader to believe that the thing is, to say the least, of it, possible. Otherwise, you will be in the position of a man who tries to prove the beauty of the aforesaid sunset to an audience who is probably convinced that there is no such thing as the sun."

Now, the second: As faith in God, so peace on earth has its source in the heart of the individual.

Peace is the price of eternal vigilance and constant righteous efforts. A noble and god-like character is not a thing of favour or chance, but is a natural result of continued effort and right thinking, the effect of long-cherished association with god-like thoughts. An ignoble and bestial character by the same process is the result of the continued harbouring of grovelling thoughts. " Man is made or unmade by himself. In the armoury of thought he forges weapons by which he destroys himself; he also fashions the tools with which he builds for himself heavenly mansions of joy and strength, and peace."

That is the message of the Saviour. From the heart comes good thoughts and bad thoughts: " By the right choice, and through application of thought, man ascends to Divine Perfection; by the abuse and wrong application of thought, he descends below the level of the beasts. Between these two extremes are all the grades of character and man is their maker and master."

The Scotch bard who knew by experience what he was talking about, said:

" Nae treasures, nor pleasures,
   Could make us happy lang;
   The heart ay's the part ay
   That makes us right or wrong."

The peace taught by the Saviour refers to the individual just as much as it does to communities. That man is not at peace who is untrue to the whisperings of Christ, and the promptings of his conscience. He cannot be at peace when he is untrue to his better self, when he transgresses the law of righteousness, either in dealing with himself in indulging in passion, or in appetites, yielding to the temptations of the flesh, or whether he is untrue to trust, transgressing the law of righteousness in dealing with his fellowmen. Peace does not come to the transgressor of law. Peace comes by obedience to law, and it is that message which Jesus would have us proclaim among men—peace to the individual that he may be at peace with his God; perfect harmony existing between himself and law, the righteous laws to which he is subject and from which he never can escape; peace in the home, families living at peace with their neighbours, exempt from family and neighbourhood brawls; striving to be exempt from the petty jealousies, petty aspirations and ambitions that come into the home and bring discard and unhappiness; peace in the families between fathers and children, mothers and fathers, husbands and wives.

Jesus taught that from within the heart of man come evil thoughts, sexual vice, acts of thefts, murder, adultery, greed. When men commit these crimes individually or collectively they trespass upon human rights and, of course, bring misery into the world. Greed prompts the accumulation of wealth even at the sacrifice of human life. What a different world this would be if men would accumulate wealth not as an end, but as a means of blessing human beings and improving human relations. A Christian conception of the right and value of human soul would have prevented the slaughter that is at this moment being perpetrated in various parts of the world. A war of aggression is barbarous, whatever the pretext may be!

Brotherhood involves service and not conquest. It involves confidence in man, in your brother; not suspicion and hatred. It involves truthful dealings; not chicanery and fraud. As fundamental to brotherhood and peace, Jesus recognized the rights of every man. When asked: Is it lawful to give tribute to Caesar, He said: " Bring me a penny, that I may see it. Whose image and superscription has it? " " And they said unto Him ' Caesar's '." Said He: " Render to Caesar the things that are Caesar's, and to God the things that are God's."

It is the spirit of brotherhood in the cheer of Christmas that makes it so glorious. Brotherliness is but the manifestation of the spirit of Christ. Thank heaven for the spirit of Christmas that brings us closer to each other in expression of such brotherhood.

Then let us pray that come it may,
(As come it will for a' that)
That Sense and Worth o'er a' the earth,
Shall bear the gree, an' a' that!
For a' that and a' that,
It's comin' yet for a' that
That man to man the world o'er
Shall brithers be for a' that."

There are those who say that if Christ were here to-day, he would not give the same teachings which He gave two thousand years ago; that His teachings were not applicable to modern-day conditions. How do men know this, since true Christianity has never been actually tested by any nation or nations?

Consider with me a few of His basic doctrines. Fundamental in all of Christ's teachings was the crime of wrong-thinking. He condemned avarice, enmity, and jealousy in the mind as vehemently as He did the results that avarice, enmity and jealousy produce. Modern psychology proves the virtue of such teachings. It confirms also His teachings regarding the injury that follows the harbouring of hate. He who harbours hatred and bitterness injures himself far more than the one towards whom he manifests these evil propensities.

Equally applicable to present conditions are His teachings regarding the value and sacredness of human life, the virtue of forgiveness, the necessity of fair-dealing, the crime of hyprocisy, the sin of covetousness, the saving power of love, the immortality of man.

His teachings regarding arbitration as a means of settling difficulties if applied by warring nations, would do away with war.

" If thou bring thy gift to the altar, and there rememberest that thy brother hath ought against thee;

" Leave there thy gift before the altar, and go thy way; first be reconciled to thy brother, and then come and offer thy gift."

So also is the paradoxical saying, " He who would save his life shall lose it, but whosoever loses his life for my sake shall find it." " Not everyone that saith 'Lord, Lord' shall enter the kingdom of heaven, but he that doeth the will of my Father which is in heaven," is an eternal truth, eternally applicable.

One man, speaking of the necessity of men's uniting to establish the Kingdom of God, says: " Such a Church will pledge its members to dedicate their lives, their fortunes and their sacred honour to the redemption of humanity from sin and ignorance. It will be an army for human salvation, working, however, not with the blare of trumpets, but quietly with adequate knowledge, with unfaltering faith in God, and with unlimited love toward men . . . It will co-operate with all men of good will in the work of redeeming men everywhere from ignorance, impoverishmnt, hate, irrational fear, foolish pride, brutal lusts, vice, crime, and self-will, whether those who so work, work under the banner of the Church in some other way."

And then he adds: " Such a Church may never arrive. But if not, the cause of Christ will perish from the earth, and with it the civilization which has fostered us."

Brethren and sisters, let me in all humility and sincerity declare to you and to the world that this Church has already arrived. It is the Church of Jesus Christ of Latter-day Saints, the mission of which is to establish peace. The living Christ is

(Continued on page 194.)

" Glory To God."—From page 182.

We send greetings and our heartfelt appreciation to the many faithful members and friends who have carried on and cared for the church work so well during the past few trying and busy years. We have made progress. But the efforts of the many have in some respects been nullified, at least in part, because of the jealousies and petty differences which have been allowed to creep into the thoughts and actions of others. Some of us have forgotten the Christmas message of " good will toward men," which should always be with us.

The strong are willing to face the facts and have the backbone to correct their errors. There has been a tendency, especially since the departure of our missionaries, for a few of our members and friends to gossip, to criticize and question various actions of their brothers and sisters. These actions are their excuse to neglect their duties in the Church, and keep them from attending services. They are tearerdowners, not builder-upers. They don't intend their actions to be such, but faultfinding is contagious. In the pursuit of fault-finding we overlook the better qualities of our fellows and put stumblingblocks in our path as well as in the path of those we confide in.

Let us all make this a time for us to renew our covenants and remember that constructive criticism is good for any cause, but idle talk by one does more harm than the ardent work of many. Before criticizing our fellow members and church workers, let us examine ourselves carefully and honestly and see that we are not more guilty than they.

" And why beholdest thou the mote that is in thy brother's eye, but considerest not the beam that is in thine own eye? "

President Heber J. Grant once said: " We generally have better Saints when the devil is barking." This I know to be true, when the devil is working on the outs.de. But the devil himself knows when he can get his licks in on the inside, he gets greater satisfaction. Let's fool him.

Now that this is off my mind, my wife and family join with me in wishing you all the compliments of the Christmas season, and may we thank God with full hearts for the measure of peace and safety we enjoy in this beautiful land. We also send our greetings to those fine young men and women who, because of their patriotic response are serving their country away from home and loved ones.; may God guard and protect them and comfort and cheer those loved ones who remain at home, and once again our deep appreciation to those many, many faithful and true members and friends who have done so much to lighten our responsible position here in South Africa.

We earnestly join with you all in singing " Glory to God in the highest and on earth peace, good will toward men."

—— ▢ ▢ ——

" I do the very best I know how—the very best I can—and I mean to keep doing so until the end. If the end brings me out all right, what is said against me won't amount to anything. If the end brings me out wrong, ten angels swearing I was right would make no difference."

—Abraham Lincoln.

Honour and shame from no condition rise,
Act well your part, there all the honour lies.
—Pope.

How The Pioneers Celebrated Christmas.—From page 187.

the managers, which was responded to by 500 voices. After benediction from Father Cahoon, the assembly retired, much gratified with their Christmas festival, which was the best they had ever witnessed.

In some of the communities of the Saints there were not enough food supplies to furnish the tables. Despite this shortage there was always a determined effort to celebrate Christmas in a suitable manner and make it the outstanding festival of the year. Such a spirit was manifest by the first settlers in Rockport Ward in Summit Stake.

The few families who moved to that region had taken but few cattle with them that season. At Christmas time they prepared a co-operative or community dinner. In the Church record we read that " the men jointly purchsed a piece of beef for which they agreed to pay in grain after the following harvest."

Thus was the spirit of Christmas kept alive by the Pioneers, no matter how limited their resources were.

—From *The Improvement Era.*

Word from the British Isles brings us the sad news of the death, in a flying accident on the 10th of September last, of Sergt-Pilot Douglas A. Camm.   His friends in South Africa send their sincere sympathies to his wife, child, mother and members of his family.   Readers of the *Messenger* will remember Brother Camm as the R.A.F. member who wrote a couple of excellent faith-promoting articles while he was stationed in Rhodesia.   He also visited Cape Town for a few days on his way to England.

District President J. Goulden Evans, of the Transvaal, is now on leave of absence from his company, doing some special work at Pofadder, Cape Province.

Brother and Sister Edgar E. Seeman, of Robert's Heights, spent their vacation at Port Alfred.

Sister Janet Brummer (wife of Brother William H.), of Newlands, is now recovering from a major operation.

We are pleased to learn that Brother Joseph M. Escojido, of the Transvaal, is now recovering from a serious illness.

Sister Doreen Brebner, of Johannesburg, took to her bed with the quincy, after her holiday to the Cape. We trust that she has fully recovered before now.

Our hearty congratulations to Brother and Sister Francis M. Donly, of the Ramah Branch Presidency, on the birth of another fine boy.   Alma Wadeson Donly was born on the 12th of November.   We understand that both mother and babe are doing nicely, and dad feels fine.

" Man bites dog," real news—sneak thieves break into " Ramah " and steal Relief Society sewing.   Not very good thanks for an association of women who work hard all year to accumulate materials to sell to raise funds to assist the needy. We hope that some needy person or persons get the benefit of the take, otherwise we label the culprit " The Meanest Thief of the Year."

Sister " Peggie " Millen Jennings and Sister Evanine Stark (daughter of Brother and Sister " Bob " Stark), of Johannesburg, visited Durban during November.

Mr. M. L. Kelly, husband of Sister Hilda Kelly, of Johannesburg, visited the Cape with the Chu Chin Chow Company.   Mr. Kelly plays the flute and piccolo in the Charles Manning Orchestra.

Springs Branch held a closing social and Relief Society sale on the 14th of November.   The numerous small babies in that branch did not stop the mothers from carrying on in the work. " Grandma " Cora Futter did an excellent job of sewing and toy making, as did the others.

Springs Branch welcomed Brother Johan Stemmet, his wife and daughter to their midst, from Robertson.

Quick work and a cool head on the part of Sister Mavis Louw, of Springs, probably saved the life of their baby. Little sister, Marlene, gave baby a full bottle of paragoric while mother wasn't looking.

Members and friends of Sister Matilda D. Allen (" Tilly "), of Mowbray, extend to her and her young son Tommy, their sincere condolence on the occasion of the death of her husband.   Mr. Thomas Allen died after a two months' illness on the 18th of November.

" Cumorah " was pleased to see Sister Hendrina G. Gows, while she was on leave at the Cape

Sister Margurita Herboldt has again returned to the hospital. We trust that she will soon recover from her painful illness.

We regret to learn that Sister Hester Gilmour, of Muizenberg, in addition to her previous illness, has found it necessary to undergo a very painful operation for the removal of a growth over her eye. We are certain that she will have a speedy recovery.

Like old times at " Cumorah " to have Sister Johanna J. Smith back home after an extended stay with daughter and husband at Durban.

The Mowbray Relief Society's closing dinner and dance on the 28th of November was a very pleasing affair and well attended. The ladies of that association have done a fine job of work during the past year.

We are always very happy to hear from the " boys " up North. We are anxious about them during these exciting and dangerous times. We are happy to report that we have heard from several of them just recently and they wish to be remembered to their friends and extend to all their best wishes for a happy Christmas. Among those we have had letters from during the past few weeks are Bobby Smith, Havelock Trollip and Dick Fagan.

To recuperate after a siege of illness, Sister H. M. McCathie, of Pietermaritzburg, has gone to Deepdale.

The close observer will notice that we have a couple of new headings, one for the Highlights and one for The Last Laugh. He will also notice that they were drawn by our old artist and former missionary, Elder Scott Whitaker. We thank Elder Whitaker for his thoughtfulness in sending these drawings and also for the fine letter. Friends and members will be glad to know that Elder Whitaker and his wife are enjoying good health. He is working in an aircraft factory in Los Angeles.

Our people of this mission will be pleased to know that the United States Government has recognized the greatness of our Pioneer leader. On the 18th of August last, a new Liberty Ship was launched. Mrs. Emma Lucy Gates Bowen, of Salt Lake City, grand-daughter of Brigham Young, christened the ship, after the name " Brigham Young " had been given to it.

We are also pleased to learn that the " Mormon Battalion " is again in the service of its country. This time in the United States Marines. There is now an entire battalion of three platoons, or one hundred and eighty-nine men, all members of the Church.

The Message Unheeded.—From page 191.

its head.   Under Him a hundred and fifty thousand men, and more, are divinely authorized to represent Him in various assigned positions.   It is the duty of these representatives to manifest brotherly love first toward one another, and then toward all mankind. To seek unity, harmony, and peace in organizations within the Church; and, then, by precept and example, to extend these virtues throughout the world.

May each Christmas find the members of the Church truer, purer, and nobler than the last, that they with intellects and hearts united may hasten the day when, as the Doctrine and Covenants says, " The Lord will bless His people with peace, that they may lift up an ensign of peace, and make a proclamation for peace unto the ends of the earth."

I conclude with this prayer of Van Dyke's :

" O Lord, our God, Thy mighty hand
    Hath made our country free ;
From all her broad and happy land
    May worship rise to Thee.
Fulfil the promise of her youth,
    Her Liberty defend ;
By law and order, love and truth,
    America befriend !

Through all the waiting land proclaim
    The Gospel of good will ;
And may the joy of Jesus' name
    In every bosom thrill.
O'er hill and vale, from sea to sea
    Thy holy reign extend ;
By faith and hope and charity
    America defend ! "

May God's peace abide in your hearts and in the hearts of people everywhere as they draw near to Him in prayer, supplication, humility, and praise this Christmastide, I pray in the name of Jesus Christ, Amen.

Cynthia Knew.

Teacher: "Cynthia, do you know 'How Doth the Little Busy Bee'?"
Cynthia (whose father, Brother Eric Jakins, has had experience with bees): "No, I only know that he doth it."

Do You "Tumble"?

"What kind of leather makes the best shoes?"
"Don't know, but banana skins make the best slippers."

Won't Stay Put.

"Do you know that your wife is telling around that you can't keep her in clothes?"
"That's nothing. I bought her a home, and I can't keep her in that either."

War News.

"What's the trouble in Wombat's house?"
"Wombat accuses his wife of using dumdum biscuits."

Not Bad Enough.

The host: "It's beginning to rain; you'd better stay for dinner."
The guest: "Oh, thank you very much; but it's not bad enough for that."

Physiology.

Teacher: "Now who can tell me where is the home of the swallow?"
Arthur: "The home of the swallow is in the stommick."

Co-operation.

Mary: "And did you let him kiss you?"
Kay: "Let him? I had to help him!"

Very, Very Good.

"I'm going away for good!"
"Going away for good?"
"Yes, going away for good."
"Good!"

Unprejudiced.

It was during the impanelling of a jury that the following colloquy occurred:
"You are a property holder?"
"Yes, Your Honour."
"Married or single?"
"I have been married five years, Your Honour."
"Have you formed or expressed an opinion?"
"Not for five years, Your Honour."

Large Family.

During the visit of one of the British convoys, an English Tommy was telling of the large family he came from and made the following remark:
"Yes'm. And the funny thing is that all the names begin with a 'haitch.' There's 'Orace,' 'Erbert,' 'Enry,' 'Ugh,' 'Ubert,' 'Arold,' and 'Arriet'—all except the last one and we 'ad 'er named Halice."

Kaye Was Too High Toned.

A few weeks after Kay Evans started to sign her name "Kaye," Brother Harvey wrote her the following note:
"Dear Keye: Dade and Mome have gone to visit Aunt Joe. Uncle Ariele is buying a new machine, but doesn't know whether to get a Cheve or a Forde. The cowe had a calfe, and I was going to call it Joye but changed it to Jime, because it was a bulle. Your loving brother, Harve."

The Answer.

"Uncle," said the earnest young man, "I am desperately in love with a lovely young girl. How can I learn what she really thinks of me?"
"Marry her, my boy, marry her!"

Hardly Fills the Bill.

Bob: "This is a splendid suit. I've nothing but praise for my tailor!"
Robbie: "So he told me."

Health Note.

Teacher: "Tommy, what is meant by nutritious food?"
Tommy: "Something to eat that ain't got no taste to it."

Forgiveness.—From page 189.

brethren, and their sin; for they did unto thee evil: and now, we pray thee, forgive the trespass of the servants of the God of thy father.   And Joseph wept when they spake unto him.

" And his brethren also went and fell down before his face; and they said, Behold, we be thy servants.

" And Joseph said unto them, Fear not: for am I in the place of God?

" But as for you, ye thought evil against me; but God meant it unto good, to bring to pass, as it is this day, to save much people alive."

Blessed is the man or the woman that does not hold grudges!

—HAROLD K WELCH—

And she brought forth her firstborn son and wrapped him in swaddling clothes, and laid him in a manger . . .

And there were in the same country shepherds abiding in the field, keeping watch over their flock by night.

And lo, the angel of the Lord came upon them, and the glory of the Lord shone round about them; and they were sore afraid.

And the angel said unto them, Fear not: for behold, I bring you good tidings of great joy, which shall be to all people.

For unto you is born this day in the city of David a Saviour, which is Christ the Lord.

And this shall be a sign unto you; Ye shall find the babe wrapped in swaddling clothes, lying in a manger.

And suddenly there was with the angel a multitude of the heavenly host praising God, and saying

GLORY TO GOD IN THE HIGHEST, AND ON EARTH PEACE, GOOD WILL TOWARD MEN.

———

PEACE I LEAVE WITH YOU, MY PEACE I GIVE UNTO YOU: NOT AS THE WORLD GIVETH, GIVE I UNTO YOU.   LET NOT YOUR HEART BE TROUBLED, NEITHER LET IT BE AFRAID.

CPSIA information can be obtained
at www.ICGtesting.com
Printed in the USA
BVHW082306191118
533509BV00032B/5204/P

9 781333 967260